Teach me How to Pray Salah

Teaching Muslim Kids the Salat Prayer

BY THE SINCERE SEEKER **KIDS** COLLECTION

Peace be upon you! My name is Amin, and my name is Saba. We are brother and sister.

Congratulations on deciding to learn to pray! We want you to take a journey with us where we teach you to pray step by step, so you can learn how to communicate with Allah, your Creator!

But first, what is the Salah Prayer, and why do we do it? Praying to Allah is the second pillar of Islam. We believe in and worship Allah, our Creator. He is the Creator of you and me and this whole world. We worship Allah because He is worthy of worship and to thank Him. We pray to Him five times daily.

Salah is our way of connecting with Allah throughout the day, so we can build a good relationship with the One who created us and loves us so much! When we pray, we ask Allah for guidance to show us the straight path to living a good life in this world and the next.

Prophet Muhammad, peace be upon him, stated, *'Pray as you have seen me praying.'* So, we should pray the way Prophet Muhammad, peace be upon him, instructed us to pray. Muslims are required to pray to Allah five times daily. There are optional prayers throughout the day to strengthen the connection with Allah.

Here is a list of the five prayers and how many units in each:

- The first is the **Fajr** Prayer, prayed from dawn to the right before sunrise. The Fajr prayer has two units.
- The second is the **Zhuhr** Prayer, prayed just after noon (mid-day, when the sun passes the median point in the sky). The Zhur prayer has four units.
- The third is the **Asr** Prayer, prayed during the afternoon (halfway between noon and sunset). The Asr prayer has four units.
- The fourth is the **Maghrib** Prayer, prayed directly after sunset. The Maghrib prayer has three units.
- The fifth is the **Isha** Prayer, prayed late evening, during the dark of the night (approximately an hour and a half after sunset). The Isha prayer has four units.

It's important that Muslims clean their bodies, wear clean clothing, and have a clean area to pray. Before you start your prayer, you must first purify your body by performing Wudu– a cleansing Muslims perform with water before praying. Muslims must also cover their awrah when praying. For men, this is their body parts from the navel to the knees. For women, this includes their whole body except their faces and hands. Then you must face the Qibla, the direction of Mecca, where the Holy House of God, known as the Kaaba, is located.

You are ready to start your praying! I'm excited for you, so let's begin! Let's pray two units together! You start by setting an intention in your heart for the prayer you are about to perform. Then raise both your hands to your shoulder or ear height. But do not place your hands together; instead, keep them and your feet shoulder apart, and say Allah Akhbar, which translates to Allah is Greater. Keep your eyes looking down at the ground, and do not look around as it would disturb you from your prayers. Then you place your right hand over your left hand on your lower chest area. Then you recite the opening dua supplication known in Arabic as Dua Al Istiftah. This is a sunnah to recite, so it's optional, and there is no harm in skipping it. You will say:

سُبْحَانَكَ اللَّهُمَّ وَبِحَمْدِكَ وَتَبَارَكَ اسْمُكَ وَتَعَالَى جَدُّكَ وَلاَ إِلَهَ غَيْرُكَ

Subhanak Allahuma wa bihamdika tabarakasmuka wa ta'ala jadduka wa la ilaha ghairuk

Glory and praise be to You, O Allah. Blessed be Your name, and exalted be Your majesty; there is none worthy of worship except You.

Then we seek refuge in Allah from the cursed Shaytan (Satan) by saying:

أَعُوذُ بِاللهِ مِنَ الشَّيْطَانِ الرَّجِيْمِ

A`oodhu billahi min ash-Shaytanir-rajeem

I seek refuge in Allah from Satan, the accursed.

Then we say:

بِسْمِ ٱللهِ ٱلرَّحْمَٰنِ ٱلرَّحِيمِ

Bi-smi llāhi r-raḥmāni r-raḥīm

In the Name of Allah—the Most Compassionate, Most Merciful.

Then we recite the first chapter of the Holy Quran called Surat Al-Fatiha (the Opener):

ٱلْحَمْدُ لِلَّهِ رَبِّ ٱلْعَٰلَمِينَ

Alhamdu lillaahi Rabbil 'aalameen

All praise is for Allah—Lord of all worlds

ٱلرَّحْمَٰنِ ٱلرَّحِيمِ

Ar-Rahmaanir-Raheem the Most Compassionate, Most Merciful

مَٰلِكِ يَوْمِ ٱلدِّينِ

Maaliki Yawmid-Deen

Master of the Day of Judgment

إِيَّاكَ نَعْبُدُ وَإِيَّاكَ نَسْتَعِينُ

Iyyaaka na'budu wa Iyyaaka nasta'een

You alone we worship, and You alone we ask for help

اَهْدِنَا ٱلصِّرَٰطَ ٱلْمُسْتَقِيمَ

Ihdinas-Siraatal-Mustaqeem

Guide us along the Straight Path

صِرَٰطَ ٱلَّذِينَ أَنْعَمْتَ عَلَيْهِمْ غَيْرِ ٱلْمَغْضُوبِ عَلَيْهِمْ وَلَا ٱلضَّآلِّينَ

Siraatal-latheena an'amta 'alaihim ghayril-maghdoobi 'alaihim wa lad-daaalleen

The Path of those You have blessed—not those You are displeased with or those who went astray.

Then we say:

امين

Ameen

(Here you are asking Allah to accept your dua supplication)

Then it is Sunnah to read a short Chapter or a few Verses of your choice from the Holy Quran.

You raise your hands to your shoulder or ear length and say Allah Akhbar (Allah is Greater) while going into a bowing position with both your hands on your knees, fingers spread a little, your back and head lined up straight, your elbows raised and tucked in and not outward, and say at least one time silently (three is recommended):

سُبْحَانَ رَبِّيَ الْعَظِيمِ

Subhaana Rabbiyal-'Adheem

Glory to my Lord the Exalted

Then rise while raising both your hands to your shoulder or ear length once and say:

سَمِعَ اللهُ لِمَن حمِده، ربَّنا ولك الحمدُ

Sami Allahu liman Hamidah, Rabbana Wa Lakal Hamd

Allah Hears Whoever Praises Him - Oh Our Lord, All Praise is to You

Then you slightly pause for a second.

Then you fall into prostration while saying Allah Akhbar (God is Greater). Place your forehead on the ground. The seven body parts that should touch the ground include your face with your nose, two hands, two knees, and two feet– all pointing forward. Do not place your elbows on the floor; instead, keep them pointed up inwards, and do not rest your stomach on your thighs. Keep from sitting on your stomach to the best of your ability. While in prostration (called sujood in Arabic), say silently at least once (three is recommended):

سُبْحَانَ رَبِّيَ الأَعْلَى
Subhana Rabbi Al Ala
Glory be to my Lord, the Most-High

Then you rise from your prostration position while saying Allah Akhbar (God is Greater) with your knees bent and palms placed on your thighs near your knees. Your right foot should be straight, and you will sit on your left foot, keeping it horizontal to the ground while saying twice silently:

رَبِّ اغْفِرْ لِي

Rabbighfir lee
Lord, forgive me

Then prostrate yourself to the ground again while saying Allah Akhbar (God is Greater) and repeat the same words on the prostration page, which again are:

سُبْحَانَ رَبِّيَ الأَعْلَى
Subhana Rabbi Al Ala
Glory be to my Lord, the Most-High

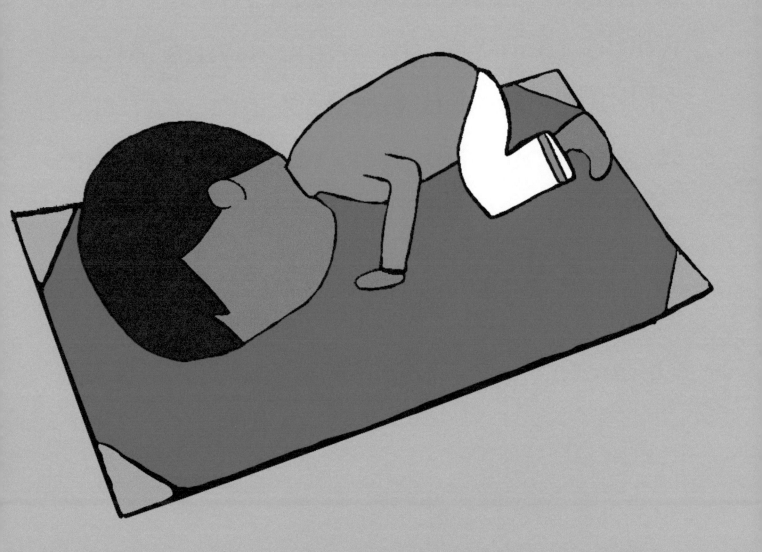

After this, you have completed one unit of prayer called Rak'ah in Arabic. You would then get up while saying Allah Akhhbar (God is Greater) and pray the second unit of prayer, repeating all the same steps outlined above, starting from reciting the first chapter of the Holy Quran called Surat Al-Fatiha (the Opener).

After finishing two units of prayer, remain sitting on your knees with your hands on your thighs near your knees. You will sit on your left foot, keeping it horizontal with your right foot straight up vertically and your toes pointing toward the Qibla (Mecca). With your right hand, point your index finger towards the Qibla (towards Mecca, the direction we pray), making a circle with your thumb and middle finger, or you can make a fist with all your fingers except for your index finger, which should be pointed. You can keep your pointed finger still or slightly move it up and down. Look down at your finger or in the area where your head was and recite silently what is known as the Tashahhud:

التَّحِيَّاتُ لِلهِ وَالصَّلَوَاتُ وَالطَّيِّبَاتُ السَّلَامُ عَلَيْكَ أَيُّهَا النَّبِيُّ وَرَحْمَةُ اللهِ وَبَرَكَاتُهُ السَّلَامُ عَلَيْنَا وَعَلَى عِبَادِ اللهِ الصَّالِحِينَ أَشْهَدُ أَنْ لاَ إِلَهَ إِلاَّ اللهُ وَأَشْهَدُ أَنَّ مُحَمَّدًا عَبْدُهُ وَرَسُولُهُ

At-tahiyyatu lillahi was-salawatu wat-tayyibat, as-salamu alaika ayyuhan-Nabiyyu wa rahmatAllahi wa baraktuhu. As-salamu alaina wa ala ibad illahis-salihin, ashahdu an la illaha ill-Allah wa ashhadu anna Muhammadan abduhu wa rasuluhu

All compliments, prayers, and beautiful expressions are for God. Peace be on you, O Prophet, and Allah's mercy and blessings are on you. And peace be on us and Allah's good, pious worshipers. I bear that no one has the right to be worshipped except Allah and that Muhammad is His slave and Apostle.

Then you recite what is known as the Dua Al-Ibrahimiya (The Prayer of Ibrahim):

اَللّٰهُمَّ صَلِّ عَلَىٰ مُحَمَّدٍ وَعَلَىٰ آلِ مُحَمَّدٍ كَمَا صَلَّيْتَ عَلَىٰ إِبْرَاهِيمَ وَعَلَىٰ آلِ إِبْرَاهِيمَ إِنَّكَ حَمِيدٌ مَجِيدٌ اَللّٰهُمَّ بَارِكْ عَلَىٰ مُحَمَّدٍ وَعَلَىٰ آلِ مُحَمَّدٍ كَمَا بَارَكْتَ عَلَىٰ إِبْرَاهِيمَ وَعَلَىٰ آلِ إِبْرَاهِيمَ إِنَّكَ حَمِيدٌ مَجِيدٌ

Allaahumma salli ala Muhammad wa ala aali Muhammad kama sallaita ala Ibraaheem wa ala aali Ibraaheem innaka Hameedun Majeed, wabaarik ala Muhammad wa ala aali Muhamaad kama baarakta ala Ibraaheem wa ala aali Ibraaheem innaka Hameedun Majeed.

O Allah, send your grace, honor, and mercy upon Muhammad, and upon the family of Muhammad, as You sent Your grace, honor, and mercy upon Ibrahim; you are indeed worthy of Praise, Full of Glory. O Allah, send Your blessings upon Muhammad and the family of Muhammad, as You sent Your blessings upon Ibrahim; you are indeed worthy of Praise, Full of Glory.

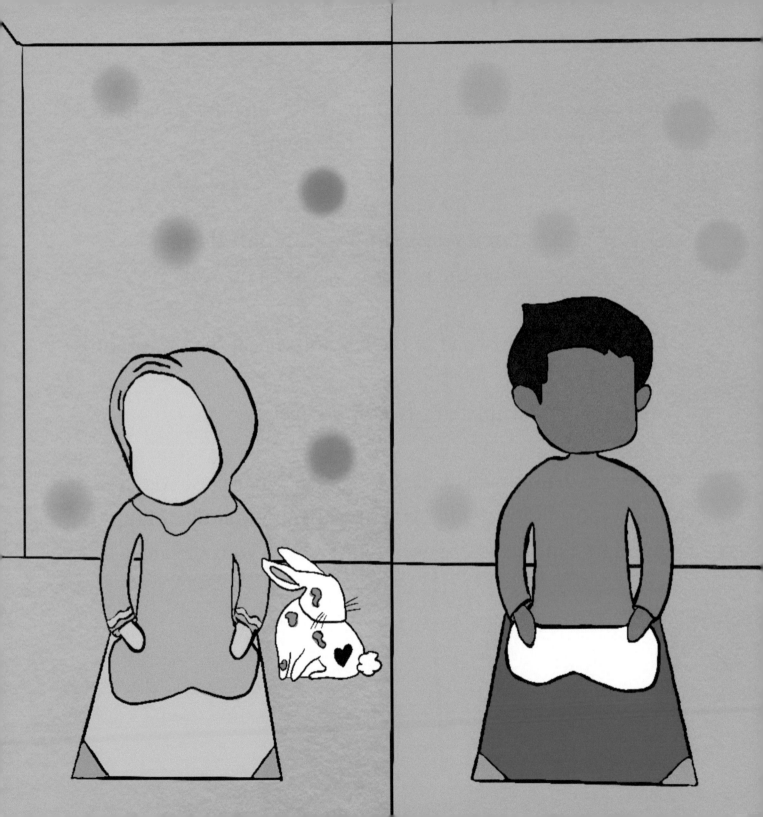

Then you would conclude your prayer by turning your head to the right first while saying:

السَّلَامُ عَلَيْكُمْ وَرَحْمَةُ اللهِ

Assalamu Alaikum Wa Rahmatullah
Peace and the mercy of Allah be on you.

Then you turn your head to the left and repeat the same words.

You have now completed a two-unit payer!

We are so happy you took this journey with us! May Allah accept your Prayers and reward you abundantly. May your prayers be a means to connect you closer to your Creator!

The End.

Made in the USA
Columbia, SC
31 October 2024

45312362R00022